FROM SEED TO PLANT

DAISY

BY GAIL GIBBONS

HOLIDAY HOUSE
NEW YORK

TOMATO

For Sue and Don Collins

Special thanks to Bob Welch
of Shearer's Greenhouses,
Bradford, Vermont

SEEDS

SQUASH

VIOLET

Copyright © 1991 by Gail Gibbons
All rights reserved
Printed and bound in July 2023 at Leo Paper,Heshan, China.

Library of Congress Cataloging-in-Publication Data

Gibbons, Gail.
From seed to plant / written and illustrated by Gail Gibbons.—
1st ed.
p. cm.
Summary: Explores the intricate relationship between seeds and
the plants which they produce.
ISBN 0-8234-0872-8
1. Seeds—Juvenile literature. 2. Plants—Juvenile literature.
3. Plants—Development—uvenile literature. [1. Seeds.
2. Germination. 3. Plants.] I. Title.
QK661.G53 1991
581.3—dc20 90-47037 CIP AC
ISBN 0-8234-1025-0 (pbk.)

ISBN-13: 978-0-8234-0872-6 (hardcover)
ISBN-13: 978-0-8234-1025-5 (paperback)

ISBN-10: 978-0-8234-0872-8 (hardcover)
ISBN-10: 978-0-8234-01025-0 (paperback)

52 54 56 58 60 59 57 55 53 51

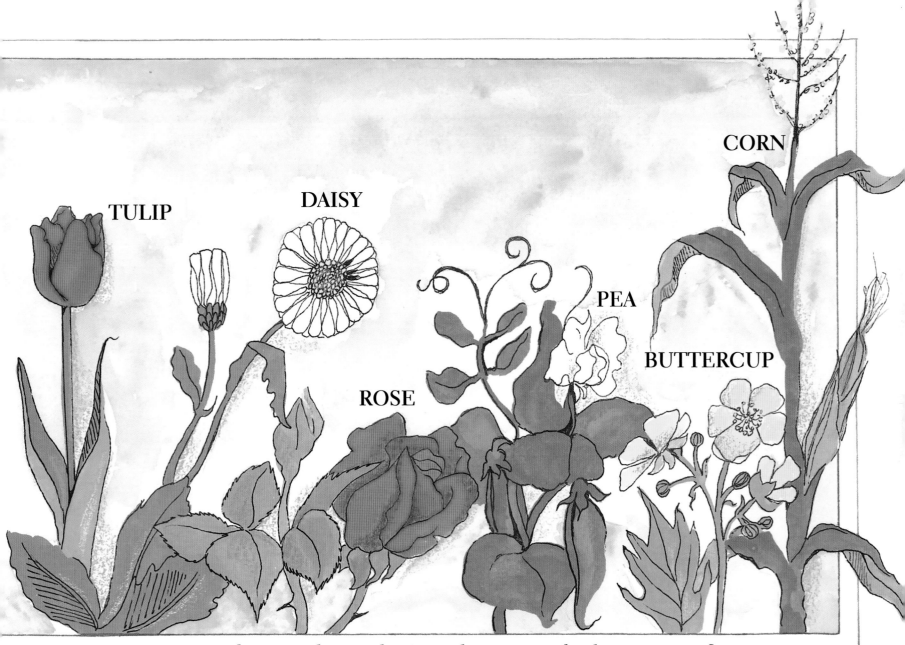

TULIP

DAISY

CORN

PEA

ROSE

BUTTERCUP

Most plants make seeds. A seed contains the beginning of a new plant.

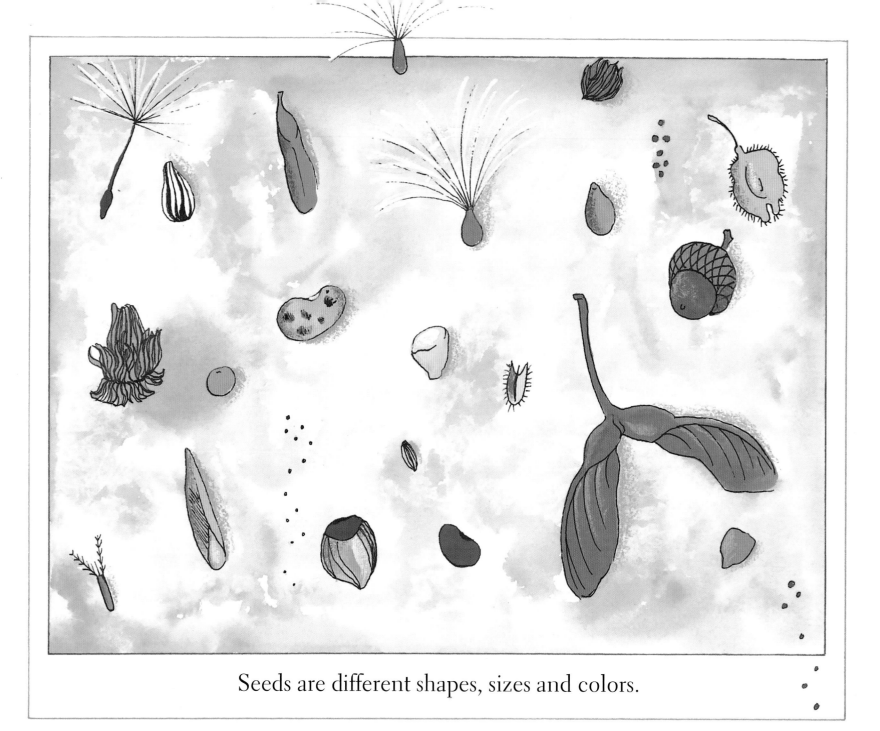

Seeds are different shapes, sizes and colors.

SUNFLOWER

OAK TREE

All seeds grow into the same kind of plant that made them.

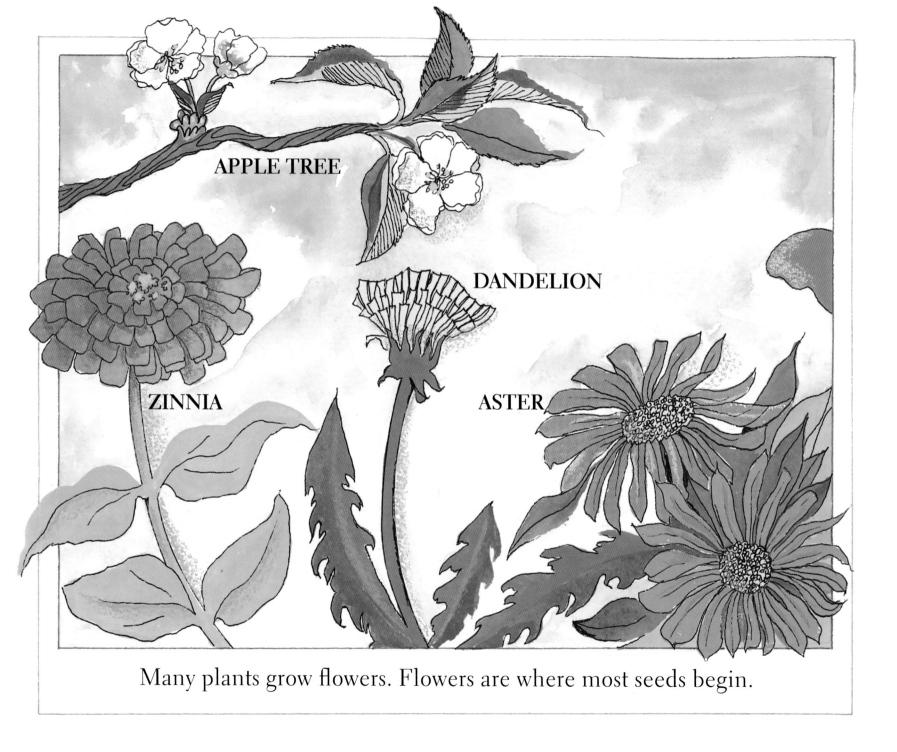

APPLE TREE

DANDELION

ZINNIA

ASTER

Many plants grow flowers. Flowers are where most seeds begin.

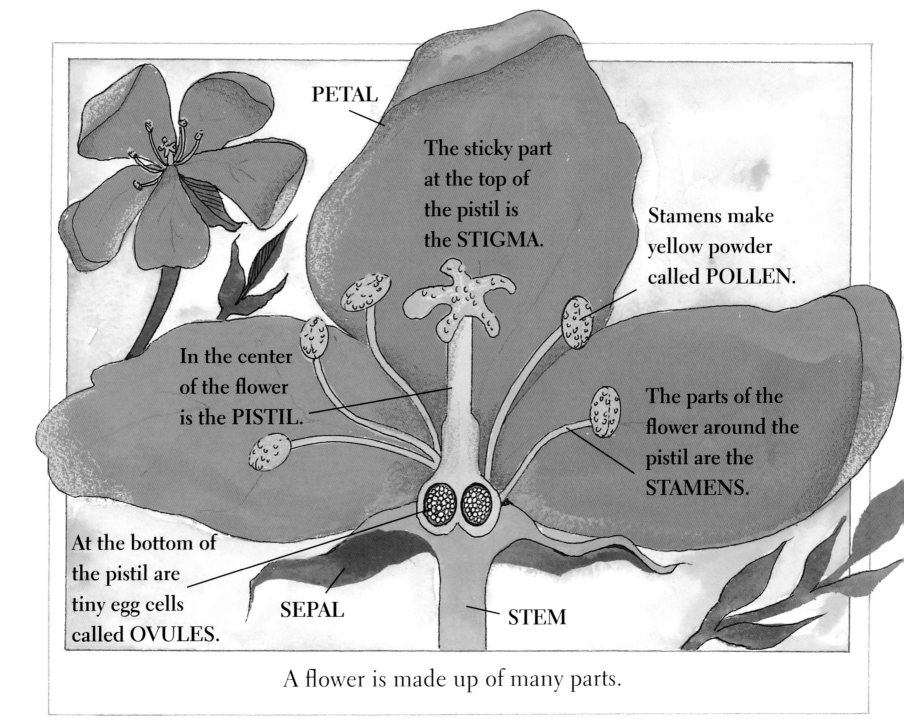

PETAL

The sticky part at the top of the pistil is the STIGMA.

Stamens make yellow powder called POLLEN.

In the center of the flower is the PISTIL.

The parts of the flower around the pistil are the STAMENS.

At the bottom of the pistil are tiny egg cells called OVULES.

SEPAL

STEM

A flower is made up of many parts.

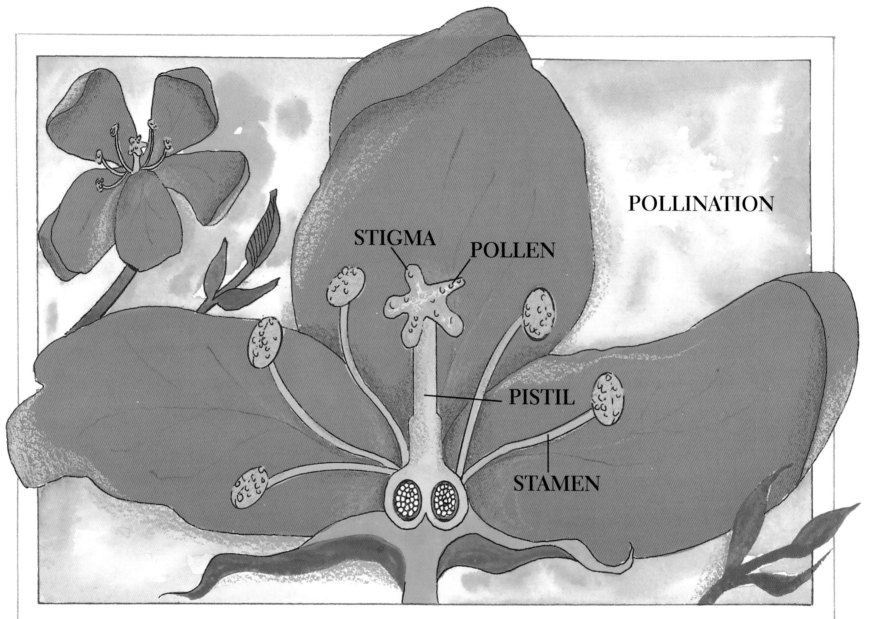

POLLINATION

STIGMA POLLEN

PISTIL

STAMEN

Before a seed can begin to grow, a grain of pollen from the stamen must land on the stigma at the top of the pistil of a flower like itself. This is called pollination.

Pollination happens in different ways. Often, win blows pollen from flower to flower.

POLLEN

POLLEN

Bees, other insects and hummingbirds help pillinate, too.
While they visit flowers for their sweet juice, called nectar,
pollen rubs onto their bodies.

Then they carry the pollen to another flower where it comes off onto its pistil.

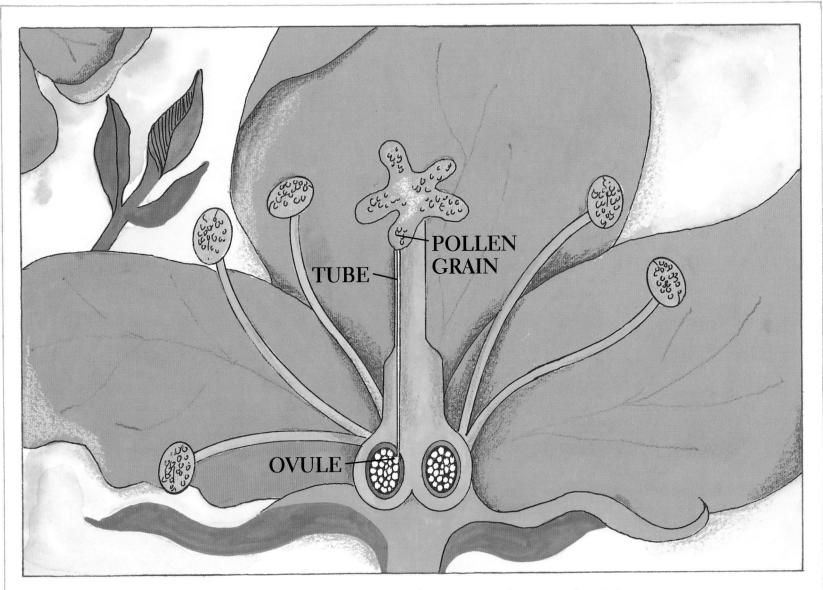

If a pollen grain from a flower lands on the pistil of the same kind of flower, it grows a long tube through the pistil into an ovule. This is the beginning of a seed.

POD

FRUIT

The seeds grow inside the flower, even as the flower begins to die. As the seeds become bigger, a fruit or pod grows around them. The fruit or pod protects the seeds.

When the fruit or pod ripens, it breaks open. The seeds are ready to become new plants.

Some seeds fall to the ground around the base of the plant where they will grow.

Some pods or fruits open and the seeds pop out. Some-
times, when birds eat berries, they drop the seeds.

Other seeds fall into streams, ponds, rivers or the ocean.
There, they travel on the water until they stick to dirt along
a shore.

The wind scatters seeds. Some seeds have fluff on them that
lets them float to the ground like tiny parachutes. Others
have wings that spin as they fall.

Animals help scatter seeds, too. They hide acorns and nuts in the ground. Some seeds have hooks that stick to the fur of animals or people's clothes. Later, they drop off onto the ground.

A flower bed or vegetable garden is beautiful! Seeds are planted to grow in the gardens.

The seeds come in small envelopes or boxes. Directions explain how to plant the seeds and care for the plants.

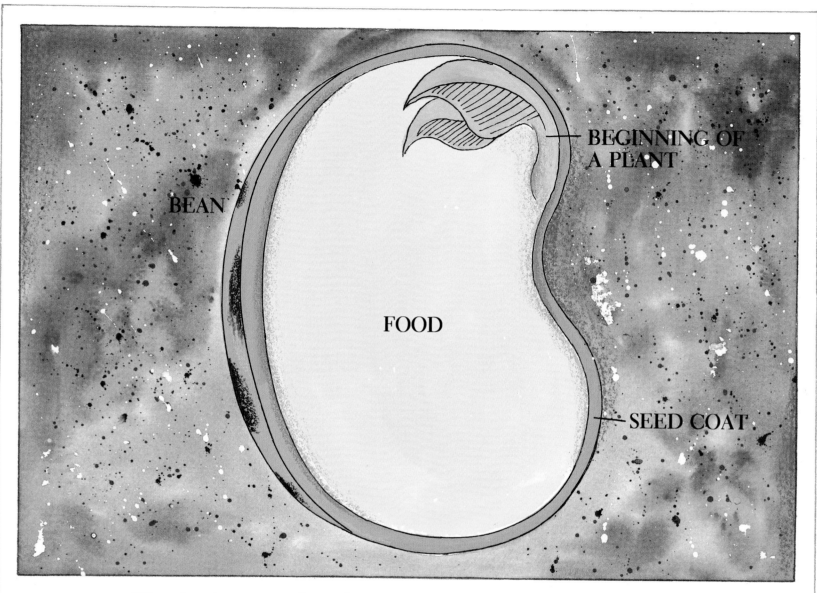

BEAN

BEGINNING OF
A PLANT

FOOD

SEED COAT

The beginning of a plant is curled up inside each seed.
Food is stored inside the seed, too. The seed has a seed coat
on the outside to protect it.

A seed will not sprout until certain things happen. First it must be on or in the soil. Then it needs rain to soak the seed and soften its seed coat.

GERMINATION

ROOT

When the sun shines and warms the ground, the seed coat breaks open and the seed begins to grow. This is called germination. A root grows down into the soil. The root takes in water and minerals from the soil for food.

Up grows a shoot. Green leaves grow up from the shoot toward the sun.

The plant grows bigger and bigger. The leaves make food for the plant from the water and minerals in the soil, the sunlight, and the air all around the plant.

BUD

Finally, the plant is full-grown. Buds on the plant open into flowers where new seeds will grow.

Many of the foods people eat are seeds, fruits and pods.
They are full of nutrition, vitamins and minerals and . . .

they are tasty, too!

A "FROM SEED TO PLANT" PROJECT

HOW TO RAISE BEAN PLANTS

1. Find a clean glass jar. Take a piece of black construction paper and roll it up.

2. Slide the paper into the jar. Fill the jar with water.

3. Wedge the bean seeds between the black paper and the glass. Put the jar in a warm place.

BEANS

4. In a few days the seeds will begin to sprout. Watch the roots grow down. The shoots will grow up.

WATCHING YOUR BEAN SEEDS WHILE THEY SPROUT

CARING FOR YOUR BEAN PLANTS

5. Put dirt into a big clay pot.

6. Carefully remove the small plants from the glass jar. Place them in the soil, covering them up to the base of their shoots.

7. Water them . . . and watch them grow!

...SEEDS & PLANTS...SEEDS & PLANTS...

 Scientists who study plants are called botanists.

 Some seeds sprout only in the heat of a forest fire.

 Some plants live for only one season. They are called annuals.

Other plants die at the end of a season but grow back the following year. They are called perennials.

 Plants in the desert, such as cactus plants, store water in their stems. They can live for a long time without rain.

 Mountain plants are short so the wind can't blow them over.

 Plants move! Many flowers open in the morning and shut at night. Some close when it rains. Also, plants move toward light.

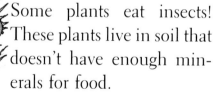 VENUS FLYTRAP — Some plants eat insects! These plants live in soil that doesn't have enough minerals for food.

 RAFFLESIA PLANT — The biggest flower in the world grows on the island of Sumatra. It can weigh up to twenty-five pounds and can be four feet across.